NEED A BIT OF FREEDOM
AND OTHER POEMS

K. Siva Reddy

NEED A BIT OF FREEDOM
AND OTHER POEMS

K. Siva Reddy

Translated from the original Telugu by
M. Sridhar and Alladi Uma

Hawakal Publishers
New Delhi | Calcutta

HAWAKAL
New Delhi | Calcutta

HAWAKAL PUBLISHERS
70 B/9 Amritpuri, East of Kailash, New Delhi 65
33/1/2 K B Sarani, Mall Road, Calcutta 80

Email info@hawakal.com
Website www.hawakal.com

Cover art by Shutterstock

Cover designed by Bitan Chakraborty

First edition(paperback) February 2021

ISBN: 978-81-948538-1-7

Price: INR 500 | USD 17.99

to

Rentala Gopalakrishna (1920-1995)

in deep respect

for spreading progressive thoughts in Telugu

as a poet, playwright and translator

OF EMPTY SPACES AND MANGO GROVES

A Note on K. Siva Reddy's Poetry

Truth is, poetry tends to be a very personal means of communication, even when it is written of universal, public concerns. One's natural 'audience' for poetry, if there is any audience for it at all, is the small group of people one knows intimately, who really care what may happen to think or feel. After all, literature is supposedly timeless and universal. Aren't we right?

K. Siva Reddy's poetry is not new to me. I have scrupulously followed his work, whenever I could, when translations of his work appeared in national magazines.

Siva Reddy's voice in these later poems is personal, concerned, with the words so common in these translations to the point of banality. But the feeling in the poem comes out cleanly, rough and raw. He is the insider, often the loser; sitting alone by the roadside, all alone and probably hating it:

"Outside the gate next to the footpath
he placed a chair and sat in the sun"

—"Outside the Gate"

In another poem, he is the one

"[...] who had filled within his body
coconut groves, mango groves, banana plantations"
—"With One Person Not Being There"

What makes Siva Reddy's voice so plain, so compelling? I would put it to a clear self-assessment devoid of any self-pity. "You in Front of Yourself" is one of those poems that demands a responsible reading:

"Sometimes
it is difficult to balance
an extra gram, on any side
turns the scales upside down
the wire will shake
it will be as if you have lost your footing
the depths below opening their mouths."

Later, in the same poem, he says:

"Sometimes the darkness of empty spaces
will swallow you up like a python
There's no knife at the navel, what will the hands do"

I must admit that the poet's inherent modesty filters into his poems, which are honestly written. Poems that stand still in the surrounding chaos, poems of direct, sympathetic statement. His metaphors are not elaborate, and yet nothing of a charged lyrical quality is lost:

"The fear will not vanish even after reaching the shore
Who is folding you into a thin tracing paper that doesn't tear"
—"It has Dawned"

Or, look at these lines from "Stone Goddess":

"The link between forgetfulness and memory
          gets snapped, everything is topsy-turvy
Which tree will respond, which flower will blossom
A stone goddess will walk right through the village."

To my mind, a nature-worshipping inwardness is clearly visible in his poems. Let us consider these lines:

"Swinging in the sky feels the same as
walking on the ploughed field, in the mud"
—"To the Sky Branch"

Elsewhere, in "If Human Beings Were Trees,"

"Maybe there is a tree inside the human being
Maybe that has sprouted like this
                    flowered like this —
. . .
A vague feeling of the roots stirring somewhere inside"

To me, Siva Reddy is a poet who uses language with the utmost care, almost as if he writes in whispers: "The dwellers of the sky will slip down to the earth / the dwellers of the earth will crawl up to the sky" ("A Farmer is Indeed a Farmer"). It seems to me the poet is somewhat reluctant to commit himself to more than this reconciling of earth and sky. Hints are what he prefers, suggestions from the border between separate identities, between the interface of psychic energies, between "hardness" and "wateriness." And how I wish I were reading his poems in the original Telugu.

Most of Siva Reddy's poems deal with the contemporary experience, and his subjects should be familiar to most of his readers. But basic to this experience is the concept that *poetry is, in itself, an experience.* His poems, I feel, make a sensory response of their own that stays with the reader long after they have been put away on the shelf.

The skimpy, meager Telugu I carry in my head tells me that Alladi Uma and M. Sridhar have quite adequately responded to the original Telugu versions.

And finally, I'd ask myself: Do I see sparks of wisdom in Siva Reddy's poems? My answer would unhesitatingly be yes, but its voice comes from the sound of only proximate matters.

Siva Reddy talks from the heart.

A humane voice indeed.

Jayanta Mahapatra

(Jayanta Mahapatra)
October 4, 2020

TRANSLATORS' NOTE

From the first collection of his poems, *Rakthan Suryudu* (1973) to the present volume *Konchem Swechchagaavaali* (2019) Siva Reddy's poetic journey has been a long march. Filling as he did when he came on the Telugu poetic scene the void of a forceful second generation of revolutionary poetry, Siva Reddy has so far published an amazing corpus of twenty seven collections. While he maintained his progressive outlook throughout, his poetry in the last two decades has gradually turned inward, become more complex, more reflective and philosophical. What K. Satchidanandan says of a poem in his "Introduction" to D. Kesava Rao's translation of his 2002 collection titled *Antarjanam* broadly applies to many of his poems since then:

> Here is an introspective, meditative poem that also takes into account what the body feels and observes thus ending the Cartesian duality between the body and the mind or spirit. The poet does not denounce physicality, but uses the body as a tool to understand the inner core of things and events; he remains part of the

> human world with all its pleasures and agonies and yet is able to observe it with detachment thus collapsing the seeing self, the feeling self and the thinking self. (*The World Within*, Hyderabad: Jhari Poetry Circle, 2012, 8.)

The present volume contains poems about very mundane matters, poems that assert his faith in the collective voice, poems that are reflections on the poetic craft, poems on old age and poems from the perspective of a grandchild, and poems that are deeply reflective of life. If anything, the poems seem to have become less complex in terms of their structure. But they are deceptively simple when one sits down to translate them. The free verse with its disregard for the punctuation marks that allows the flow of thought (except for an exclamation mark or a question mark here and there) certainly makes for an easy reading in the source, but poses problems in rendering it into English. Or how does one translate a poem like "Rendu Paadaalu" (Two Feet") where the expression, "the feet" might simultaneously stand for the physical feet as well as poetic feet? We have enjoyed the challenge of rendering them. Hope our readers will appreciate them.

We have left out from this collection the poems of Kuwar Narayan (Hindi) and Gurucharan (Punjabi) that Siva Reddy had translated into Telugu, and the poems titled "Liberty", "Maria" and "Copacabana" that he had written originally in English.

We appreciate the trust reposed in us by Siva Reddy. He gave us ample time and freedom to work on the translation.

We are grateful to Mr. Jayanta Mahapatra for making time to write a "Foreword" to this translation.

We thank *Hawakal Publishers* for coming forward to publish this book.

CONTENTS

NEED A BIT OF FREEDOM

Need a bit of freedom
        to flap the wings
to shake off the raindrops on the wings
to set right the feathers with the beak
to stretch out this leg this way, that leg that way—
to lift the head up and look at the leaves on the trees
when a raindrop falls "tup" on the head—
to widen the nostrils
and inhale the air with eyes
        when the breeze blows ever so gently—
Need a bit of freedom
to call a man a man
to call an animal an animal
Need a bit of freedom
to call a night a night
to call a day a day—

Need a bit of freedom
to flap the wings
        to fly in the air—

(Translation of "Konchem Swechchagaavaali")

BRIDGE

I have been walking
        on this bridge for the past fifty years
No change, has just become a bit fat
        grown big.
Do things too have age
        have old age?
Carrying, carrying on the burden saying they can't any longer
        do they complain, do they grieve?
Do they look forward
        to someone relieving them of the burden—
Eyes can't see
The back is bent
For the past fifty years
        is this bridge carrying me
        or am I carrying the bridge—
Laal salaams to the bridge
    that hasn't collapsed even though the back is bent.

(Translation of "Vanthena")

JUST A LITTLE MORE

I guess they deserve
just a little more
        love, respect and kindness
the aged
        not just in this country
        in any country.
But then children
Children I guess deserve
much more love, compassion,
attention, extraordinary kindness and concern—
Fluid state ought to exist
only in these two places—
        Must welcome one
        with that past affection
        with a burning heart
                for the never-ending desire for life
Must bid goodbye
to the other
with gratitude
for the life bestowed
for the opportunities left behind.

(Translation of "Inkonchem")

HE'S JUST LIKE THAT

Who is scared of life—
Will the imaginative Viswanatha
riding on a thousand winged horse
roaming the entire universe
be scared—
Will the Charaka
who mesmerizing the mud found the cure for all ills
be scared—
For him everything is a challenge
a pillar-like question
A *Yerukala*[1] man who searching every root finds answers
will he be afraid—will he retreat—
The "Vatapi jeernam" Vidura
who digesting everything
be it rock or such, kingdom or such
will not go anywhere.
He will stitch everything together—
There will be justifications, there will be corrections
there will also be those
that will have to be thrown out being sliced to pieces
going around the village touching every house mocking the fate
he will draw a circle around every man—

1 *Yerukala* refers to a tribal community in Andhra Pradesh and Telangana.

Life ought to be scared looking at man
ought to circle around the feet like a puppy
Who is afraid of life
Most importantly is the poet afraid of life
Will the poet who is the magician who makes fear frightened be afraid
Will the poet who creates the future with art as the centre be afraid
Will the man who showing the way celebrates the theppotsavam[2] be afraid
Look at his finger tips—
They are the centre of life of the races, rivers and world—
Will the poet who is a Chenchu the eternal traveller be afraid

Let it drizzle, let stones break
Let flowers shower on nights—
            He is ahead, far ahead
There will be a dog behind him
There will be dog whose pseudonym is friendship
He with a crooked stick on his shoulder
with a saddi[3] bundle—he is just like that
since the birth of time he is just like that
            he is just like that—

(Translation of "Athanalaane...")

---

2 Theppotsavam refers to the festivities of God celebrated on the waters of a temple lake.
3 Saddi is leftover food of the previous night usually mixed with buttermilk.

TO MUD

To Sikha Akash with love

Mud
has no right to die
it's damned to live
Mud that knows the beauty of labour
has no right to become dumb
has no right to remain silent.

Mud that makes
fields blossom into canals
a plough into a small field bank
has no right to reject men
Mud that waters the world
          with cupped hands
has no freedom to say it's not water.

The earth
that raises and sustains
the entire animal kingdom
the tree universe
the living and non-living things
has the right only to infuse life
has no right to take life

(Translation of "Mattiki")

CHILDREN

Children laugh looking at me
I live looking at children
        One is a morning raga
        the other an evening raga
Look at the faces of those half blossomed ones
they light up a crore of suns
they create new ever so new worlds
What can they find in this worn-out face
Do they find "Babu, look at Kasipatnam"[4]
or do they find the giant wheel of London
or do they find the mountain ranges or Himalayan peaks
or the Ganga, Brahmaputra or Kaveri rivers—
In their hands
the aroma of flowers of several thousand gardens
their body filled with the strange perfume
wafting from thousands and thousands of forest areas
caresses the world in waves and waves
        In my house
                there is a tender bud
        Tucking a flute in the waist string
        it says this is my dagger

---

4 A travelling bioscope which projects various interesting scenic pictures enjoyed primarily by children

Picking up a long stick
        it says this is my sword
Children are not just flowers
        but they must become knives, swords, daggers too

(Translation of "Pillalu")

POINTER

I know
this will lead to an "end"
        that no one can stop it—
Clenching the teeth, with toe tips
        kicking holding on to the earth
won't come out no matter how much you pull
Very difficult to pull out the snake
        that has slithered into the hole
might be cut into half
        but it will not come out
Do I have a hand in all these
Which ones can I save
        don't know if this is defeat or victory
The tussle keeps continuing—
Will the "end" frighten
The river merges finally into the ocean
The water in the canal disappears into the field
Do these finger tips now comprehend
the throb of the last moments—
He does not understand
nor does she—that they have travelled this far
dividing equally a single moment—
Does anyone understand
that the present points to the future

(Translation of "Sanketham")

THE VERY BEING

A small book in hand
like a bird
Don't have to read it, like electricity
it flows into the body—
Electricity has a language, has conversation
If you know how to read it
          poetry can be understood.
A language that has no language
A silent conversation can be understood
A book is not an ornament, it is the very being

(Translation of "Aayuvu")

ICEBERG

Doesn't Modi look great
as if frozen—like a sculpted iceberg
how much of a burden he is bearing
how much of a burden the past is
how tough it is to carry it on to the head
not letting go what has happened
installing it again and again
would he understand at least now that it is not so easy
        That killing is not infusing life
that you cannot kill something that is alive all the time
that turning history and wearing it wrong side up
will not let you breathe
that pulling back something that is moving forward
        making it static at one place is impossible
has he understood it at least now

When I look at Modi
I am reminded
of one who rolls a boulder up the hill—
When I look at Modi
I am reminded
of one who lights up a cigar
when the house is burning—

(Translation of "Manchu Raayi")

TODAY TOO

Like everyday
it dawned today too
except that its knife is
          a bit bloodstained—
Like everyday it dawned today too
Like the hand that fell into the machine
got chopped to pieces
it poured out
          blood-soaked work
When I touched the cup to the lips
to sip coffee
it smelt of boiling blood—
When I felt it would bring some bird
and place it on my palm—
it handed over
a dead cluster of things and went away
A morning
I thought fresh and dazzling
brought in depressing distorted scenes
A morning
I thought would look like a little girl's feet
a green forest
came and filled my poem

with life that had been splintered to bits—
From wherever I go to wherever I journey
no matter how many mornings I pass by
I cannot find even one word
that has no remnant of sorrow
no matter how many time periods
        come walking along
today too
at the house front
the torso keeps hanging—
Should I guess that's how it would be everyday
Should I hope someone
        would bring me a flower—

(Translation of "Ivvalakoodaa")

AMIDST A BLIND WORLD

For Dr. V. Chandrasekhara Rao

Bringing a tiny knife
a knife like a pointed blade—he stood opposite me
extend your hand and take this flower he said.
I am just a child what do I know
I said there should be no stains
there should be no blood stains
I said no tears should be shed on flowers—
This is not a flower but a knife he said
I said I don't want a knife—I want only a flower—
He moved his hands in the air
produced two eye-like flowers—
I'm one who doesn't know if it's a flower a knife or an eye—
I love flowers
I love flowers like the lips of a little girl—
As the world started producing blood-like flowers
I cried and cried and became blind—
Someone rubbed my back—made me walk amidst tombs
made me stand amidst fields
I caressed and felt
Spikelets of paddy touched my hands—
I smelt gold.
A little snake-like stream slithered past me.

Standing right there I looked towards the sky
inhaled with my nose.
When I asked for flowers they gave me knives
When I asked why knives they plucked out my eyes—
Amidst the blind world, narrating the story of suppressed races
I turned into a song-bird.

(Translation of "Andha Prapancham Madhya…")

EACH DAY

Each day a danger
each day a battle

After the state enters the forest
after the state becomes the treasure of the moneyed
becomes the magic wand
          in the hands of the capitalist
after the indigenous people
are displaced from their roots
after indigenousness and rootedness
          have been demolished
after a people's identity and lives
          have been obliterated—
in the context of the same saga
          happening all over the world
at a time when a certain uprootedness—
          is becoming universal—
Each day a danger
each day a battle

(Translation of "Eroju Karoju")

THE TWO OF THEM

On the lower step this woman
on the higher step that woman
        two dismantled carts
sons daughters-in-law
grandsons granddaughters—
a huge battalion indeed
as if there's no one in the world
as if only the two of them existed—
On the lower step this woman
on the higher step that woman
Don't know what they say to each other
Don't know how they empathize with each other?
On the branch of the neem tree up there
two crows would be cawing
a squirrel would be jumping
from this branch to that branch
as stones break
        in the sweltering sun—
as nameless wild flowers
drop down from the trees—

What have they been robbed of

(Translation of "Vaalliddaroo")

THE BOUNDARY WALL

As if "laying a foundation" for a boundary wall
I am building a fort around me
There would be no doors or windows on a boundary wall
If at all there would be a main entrance
Air and light have to enter only with permission
All those who think that a fort is a shield
will be defeated and merge with the womb of time
Where in history
are the forts, shields, guns, cannons
Which idols of the sanctum sanctorum
have become the steps beneath whose feet
The feet did not live on neither did the steps live on
If at least one lesson lives on
        if that leads us ahead
we would reach near a lake
When the people of all countries reach there
after each drinks a palmful of water
would they dig up the past, would they unearth their differences!
As a Pakistani poet said
when all the old take the doors along with them
the children will carry the windows—
When Osip Mandelstam said as he went into exile
"Let's meet again in Petersburg"

Agha Shahid Ali is saying
Let us meet again in Kashmir
In Peshawar, in Cochin, in Sultan Bazaar—
where shall we meet
then
We have to meet somewhere
When we meet we have to recognize ourselves
You me, I you—
Don't know but should there be a place where we can meet?

(Translation of "Prahareegoda")

THE HANGING

Be prepared for everything
We are walking amidst hills that are crumbling down
We are walking on roads that are suddenly breaching
We may or may not reach the other side
We are swimming in unknown rivers
As much as the eyes can see
Only as much as the hands can reach out—
There's a limit that doesn't appear as a limit
There's injustice that appears as justice
There's day that appears as night
There's night that appears as day too
Holding each bank with both hands
who is the courageous one who can cross the river slicing it like a knife
On the river-paper that cannot stand still
who will write a few lines
At a juncture when no one knows what one would do
let us be prepared for everything
Some programme has begun
to introduce us to ourselves
At the guillotine
will the poet Srinatha speak
will Siva Reddy speak
In the court that proclaims there is no guillotine

at a time when the programme
to hang you from within has begun
let us be prepared for everything

(Translation of "Uritheetha")

DID NOT RECOGNISE

He is standing under a tree and saying—
"Did not recognise"
He is standing before an animal and saying—
"Did not recognise"
He is standing before a lake and saying—
"Did not recognise"
He is standing before a house and saying—
"Did not recognise"
He is standing before a person and saying—
"Did not recognise"
He is standing before a mirror and saying—
"Did not recognise, did not recognise"

(Translation of "Gurthupattala")

HELPING HAND TO THE DISTRESSED

To Kosuru Ratnamgaru with love

Both wings are there
but they are broken
they don't help you fly.
Rice will not cook
on a stove that's turned off
Son is very much in this town
but he in this old age home
The only son in America
but he in the old age home
Old couple who can neither hear nor see
Where's home, where's the place to rest
Everyone in the same situation
those who have nothing
those who have everything
but who have been castaway at a distance
Someone's hand
is kept on the nose to reflect
"What's the use of living, better to die."
Where's the answer
to the woman who is looking keenly at me
All these people here

as if sorrows, suffering, hardships, helplessness
inability to do anything, inability to raise one's hand
about anything
lack of support, indifference, protests
piled up in a heap
what can we do
*
But there's a helping hand for the distressed
a cupped handful of gruel
a compassionate cloud
that is hovering
over everyone's head

(Translation of "Aapanna Hastham")

IT'S ONLY TO SAY I'M THERE

At this juncture
it is important to live
To be suppressed
to be dead
to vanish without a trace
to run away—
not these, not these—this is not right
A branch will break
a leaf will fall
a tear drop will move away from me
even so I must stand right here
even if fire envelops
from all four directions
even if the pen with which I am writing breaks suddenly
standing here right here
I have to choose something or the other
The line drawn by the ploughshare is a sentence
A sentence that extends to several sentences
It is important to live at this juncture
Holding the cracking body
must sojourn like a kitten
must say I am here—
must say I am alive

At this juncture it is important just to live
Just to live is a message
a struggle
It is important
not to give in but live
It is important
to hoist life like a flag
Sometimes
it is a great battle
just to say I am here

(Translation of "Nenunnaanani Cheppatame")

AN ATHEIST

An atheist entered the church
on a peaceful morning
a morning with light mild dew
when everything was absolutely calm
suddenly unexpectedly
an atheist entered the church
A very ancient Christian temple
a temple with even the dhvaja sthambham[5]
He heard the sermons of the Father
in a language he did not know
He got up and stood along with others
He said "Amen" along with others
He tried to empty his entire heart
he thought he ought to be devoid of all emotions
but that was not possible
"What would have happened to him
What would have happened to her
What weight of sorrows have they come here to unburden"
After half an hour he came out slowly
perhaps with a heavy heart
A wide world
The coolies who were going for

5 Dvaja Sthambham refers to the flagstaff at the entrance of a temple.

construction work early in the morning
        stood at the addas
tens hundreds with spades crowbars on their shoulders
with iron baskets on head—women men—for work
Their expectations
he understood
that there was nothing other than toil here
that each had to carry his burden
that each had to put up with his sorrows

[In Trichur, Kerala, an experience in a hundred year old church]

(Translation of "Nasthikudokadu")

I AM HANGING FROM A SMALL TWIG

I am hanging from a small twig of a tree
hanging from a little finger's small twig
How many worlds
can it promise and give
how many beautiful
solar power worlds can it give
how many enormously wonderful worlds can it take me to
having taken me make me accomplished
Does it know any mantras or magic
innocent pleasures surprises
With wide eyes, bright eyes
can it show golden islands—
can it completely transport me into dream-world palaces
With a tiny bit of belief
I have kept in front like a looking glass
the tender sprout of a leaf of the little twig
This is the conduit for the beautiful worlds galore
This is the little finger of the tender sprout of the tiny little twig
from which the present hangs down—
I am hanging
from a fascinated little finger
This will hide me and my generation
in the cradle of imagination
will safely take me to the other shore
What will I have there
Beauty bliss unfathomable pleasure

(Translation of "Nenoka Chirukommaku...")

NEWS OF "MODI'S YOGA WITH THE DGPS"

Shabash
A, you have learnt attentiveness
Will you teach me to carry out an encounter
with attentiveness—without dispute
Will you teach me how to give old notes
how to deceive and get new notes
Will you turn all DGPs
into magicians
To atone which sins is this yogic sleep—

This country has sunk into
a mysterious environment
Modi Swamy
shall we go back another step!

(Translation of "'DGPlatho Modi Yoga' Vaartha")

YOUR THIN FINGERS

Your thin fingers
have become even thinner
Your midrib-like thin body
has become far too thin
What sorrow has swelled up
surged over your body
Rolling you over endlessly
it has turned you into a sacred stone
You like a vine entwining from within
You like fire smouldering from within—
I can't fathom how to contain you
Saying you would crumble to pieces
if touched—
You quiver like memory
as all days of the past
drop down worried in front of you naked—
When I wake up at midnight and sit
I can't hear anything but the cricket's chirping

(Translation of "Sannani Nee Vellu")

ROOM 308

To Chandrasekhara Raogaru

Are you the pigeons'companion
or the pigeons your companions
Perhaps you alone are the companion
for the pigeons that have made a home for themselves
on the pipeline outside the window pane—
when even the wind is still
in this strange room
with strange colours with strange smell
can you hear
the room move
Someone like me keeps dropping in and out
The pigeons, you
the treetops that stand out there
beyond the window at a distance
the grey fragments of the sky
firm, determined, fearless
like an unalterable steadfast resolve—
Who doesn't know, what's there to say
Each has to mould himself
Sparkle with the knowledge of the body-matter.

[308 is the room in which Dr. V. Chandrasekhara Rao stayed for forty days in Care Hospital. I wrote this right there and read it out to him—Listening, a smile on the parched lips.]

(Translation of "Gadi 308")

THE DOG IS DREAMING

The dog is dreaming
that he has become the king of the forest
that he has become the monarch of the entire earth's surface
The dog is dreaming
that the tiger, the lion
and the rest of the animal world
is carrying him on a howdah
that his word has indeed become the law
that his knowledge alone
has become the encyclopedia
that the earth
is thrilled that everything is clean--
On one fine rainy morning
lying in the dust by the wall
in a half-asleep state
the dog is dreaming—
After looking at the rulers of many countries
no wonder the dog is dreaming like this.

(Translation of "Kukka Kalalu Kantondi")

THE SEARCH

Always
I keep a chair ready
thinking someone may drop in
in the morning when I am having tea
Even if no one turns up
won't the chair be there
One of my ancestors
may sit invisibly on it
and carry on a secret conversation
Or else
I can start a conversation
with a non-living thing
Don't non-living things have existence
Everything having an existence is a being
Are we searching
Are we longing for a fellow being
What's the difference
I can make myself sit on that chair
and have a conversation

An empty chair
will not always be empty

(Translation of "Devulaata")

THIS ONE TIME

Let this one time pass by
Calmly, cleanly,
without regrets, without atonements
Let this one time pass by
without worry about tomorrow
without confusion, without being hasty
without crises, without endless sorrow
Just this one time
I am washing and drying each time as it comes by
Just this one time at least without tears
without drought, without famine
without wretched work, without insolence
without the speeding horse dying suddenly
Just this one time
The news of yesterday irrelevant
The news of tomorrow inappropriate
Just this one time
let me change myself to myself
Hiding myself beneath my eyes
into a healthy drop
opening the door
thinking the first step
middle step, final step of a journey

ought to be the same
stop speeding
along nights, along roads
Just this one time
I on my own
as my protection—as my heaven
where no one's shadow touches
where no one's footprints fall
Just this one time, shall we make it
as mine, as yours, as all ours
shall we free it from the prison!

(Translation of "Ee Okkapoota")

BURIED BENEATH THE EARTH

A hope like a tuber buried beneath the earth
that at least at some point
either when it rains
or when the weather changes or when the earth shakes up
giving birth to a sensation
a hope
that sometime, that at least at some point
that it will sprout
like sunrise from the tuber
a hope that drives one from some corner
when one thinks there is no hope
even when all has been reduced to a wasteland
a hope that can conquer even death
How many communities, peoples of how many nations
who have experienced war, consequences of war,
hazards of war
who have suffered endless agitation, agony
those who have returned from the gallows
those who have deceived the gravedigger, the watchman
They are the ones who have
risen up bright in the presence of hope, future
What's this life except hope
a hope like dear love

A man who flings a smile on darkness
getting up and standing with limbs repeatedly coming together
even when all limbs are severed is the main lead of hope
in the journey of the human race
A bright flower that blossoms in myriad ways
is death a moment ago
Now birth—a new rebirth
Human beings, nations
          the primary source of all creation
Human being the dream foetus
will rise, rise over sunrise
will join the sky and land in one sentence

The revered poet has come to life anew
is all set to write a poetic line
Poet is a Siddhartha, poet is a Gautama Buddha

(Translation of "Bhoomilo Daagina")

BINACAGEET

A Binaca powder tin
Pencils in a plastic glass
A bronze Buddha head
Screen magazine—a radio
Two chairs, a table
Four plates, two pots
Faded panchas, torn pockets
Only these in our life-rooms
the varied freestone slabs that we have spread—
Closing almirahs
increasing cockroaches
saluting moustached tom cats
lives—lives
the gruel mud bowls that dogs licked
Scabies-sores between fingers
stench in the streets of people
A pipe without water
A bulb without a filament
Hearts that dried up
Eyes that lost sight—
Next to the park
or in the hub of the cinema hall
let us bury
our listlessness—life's worry—pangs of hunger

In fact
we are all deceived people
we are dried carcasses
stripped of skin hung upside down
For this day
two faces
the past—that past
we like coins not in use in the turmoil
as days pass by
as environment changes
only in rooms only on freestone slabs—into sleep
flowing into the lifeless-life
stitching up lips and eyes
with Binaca powder tin
with short blouses
put patches on lives
sleep don't wake up—
if you wake up you will sin
if you think you will go to hell

(Translation of "Binacageetam!")

SILENCE

He
wants silence
wants complete silence
wants pure hallowed silence
would be eighty or ninety
hollow sounds boasts, heard around
hay-like words letting out ash
sounds of clouds that travel at tremendous speed
mixed with light touched with the wetness of water—no
meaningless sounds of duplicitous nature, dry clouds—no
Words of broken hands
words of hanging pieces of meat on the string—no
The static state of water level
journeying from somewhere to somewhere—
of a bird kicking while passing by—
a syllable that trickles down from an open pair of eyes—
the wet air that wafts by from a not fully dried upper cloth
Some things are heard, some other things are seen
The low pitch of a string strummed the heart
Perhaps
the ripe age
        habituated to experience
the infinite endless surrounding silence—

He
needs a sound he alone can hear
a gift of closed eyes
After years of journey full of sound
he wishes to sleep in silence—pure silence
He needs silence

(Translation of "Nishshabdam")

WITH JUST ONE SENTENCE

With just one sentence
        I want to end
When I think in my mind
        it is just one sentence
Why extend
I think I should turn everything into a capsule and give it
To convert the entire mountain
into a pebble
why a sentence
isn't a word sufficient
to shorten it
to tighten it
        becoming heavy—
after falling in the lake
it is necessary to swim from this shore to that shore

Word is a cruel demoness
Without your being aware
        it swallows you up

(Translation of "Okka Vaakyamtho")

ABOUT THE END

Why fear about the end
        happy no matter how it ends—
Being ready for all kinds of ends
        haven't you come so far

Who will now fix clog on the hoofs
Tender feet—ought to have turned into stony hoofs
Time
what—did you think it was a handkerchief
to fold and put inside the pocket
that's a bird
        its nature
        is to fly is to pierce through

(Translation of "Mugimpu Gurinchi")

FROM WHERE

Where can I bring love from
the love of the deep waters of the earth—
the love that is evaporating progressively—
where should I bring it from—
it isn't the bent tree with ripened fruits,
        is it
to fall if you hold the trunk and shake it—
Don't know in which of the senses it is hidden
Don't know which thali bottu[6] it is holding on to
        and hanging
Don't know behind the eyes of which motherless boy it is hiding
Don't know in which turning of the road
        it died in an accident—
Perhaps it jumped off a seven storeyed building—
I have been searching since birth
to give this a shape, I am anxious
Don't know under which feet it has been trampled in this stampede
How will I be able to recognize it?
When I look at myself in the mirror
someone is peeping from behind
For dried up love
        will one find wet clues

6 Thali bottu refers to the thread tied around the neck of a bride during marriage.

Like a boy lost in the Sivaratri fair
will it sleep like an orphan on the bridge next to the road
I will ask Yerukala Singi
        for the trace of love
If I find the love that is torturing me so much
I will throttle it and bury it
        under the lime tree in my backyard

(Translation of "Yekkada Nunchi")

HUMANS WILL SURVIVE

Humans will survive
overcoming everything they will somehow survive
With steel bodies
digesting each and every mineral in the earth
with priceless bodies no force can defeat
humans will survive
Scattering all hardships like seeds
all over the world
        humans will survive
What will sorrows do
What will difficulties do
Humans who are fighting
        all kinds of battle
to survive with the sole aim of surviving
will survive growing into humongous trees walking trees
Even if they seem to slip down they don't slip down
Even if they seem to be defeated they don't get defeated
Isn't it a heroic race
Isn't it a heroic race
        that has been flowing for thousands of years
Humans turning more human
wearing invisible swords, weapons
in all four directions of the earth

spreading—extending
          expanding
burgeoning—becoming responsible
for the growth of an altogether new race

Humans will survive
With steel bodies, humans will survive.

(Translation of "Manushulu Bathukuthaaru")

IN ROCKS TOO

A small hope still
that a plant will grow amidst rocks
that an oasis will be found
in an expanding desert

Life is like that
It ends on one side
it rises up alive from the other side
No one can ever say
this is the final
    that it will end like this
Life is like that
with such extraordinary bliss
with such bottled up sorrow
with such ghastliness—
Hands will fall off
thousands and thousands of hands will sprout
Happiness that I am still alive
Pride that I am still sprouting

As if someone is digging the earth under our feet
as if the feet are caving in as roots
that no one can kill me anymore

that the secret of the entire universe
    is within me

A small hope
that we are alive
that no one can annihilate us

(Translation of "Rallalo Kooda")

TWO POETIC STATEMENTS

That old Buddha thought

Taking this fellow to school
bringing him back from school
What will others know
the quiet beauty of sounds that rules
between these two poetic statements
except those
            that have become a part of a beautiful order
What most others look upon as ordinary
are to him
activities filled with every intelligence

If looking at the world—looking at it like a yogi
is a stupendous activity
as a part of it watching
            chidren's pranks—sweet actions
experiencing them—a fulfillment of tapas
Why forests
Why bathe in fire
Why stand on a single leg
Why let your body shrivel
What you get from doing all these

you can get here effortlessly, deeply involved
It's enough
if you take a child to school
bring him back from school—
You will get what you had never experienced
            in your entire life
You will become the bee that draws honey
without sitting on the flower
Drop after drop of nectar
will accumulate in you
Finally
        you will become a food bowl

(Translation of "Rendu Kavithaavaakyaalu")

WHY THESE

What use
do poems have
Perhaps
they help me live on
            each moment
To make something or the other alive alone is their task

Birds perch on the tree on the field ridge
For the onlooker it's like the tree blossoming
Do birds enliven the tree's existence
Does the tree enliven the birds' existence
Whichever way you understand it
            in that way will you see them
They feel constrained within
Feeling constrained those that come out survive

(Translation of "Ivenduku—")

YOU IN FRONT OF YOURSELF

Sometimes
it is difficult to balance
an extra gram, on any side
    turns the scales upside down
    the wire will shake
    it will be as if you have lost your footing
    the depths below opening their mouths
Sometimes you are out of balance
Is the final decision in your hands
"Psalm of Life" will not work
    you yourself will have to sew your tear
you yourself will have to cry out your sorrow
as if the power to knot all the edges together
is not adequate, everything will be out of your hands
Sometimes the darkness of empty spaces
    will swallow you up like a python
There's no knife at the navel, what will the hands do
Helplessness will not work like balm to the eyes
Sometimes as if the entirety is dying
as if oxygen itself is fainting—
Where from should you gather the life force
There's no Nila[7] to construct a bridge
    all that has been laid has collapsed

7 Nila is supposed to have constructed the bridge for Rama to cross over to Lanka.

Anjaneya can bring the mountain
he cannot build a bridge that floats on water

Someone will bring the future
and place it obstructing the way
Unable to get rid of it, unable to jump over it
you like the sorrow-filled Rama here
you can't just let it go
you can't even poke the dead snake with a twig
you by yourself—can't even
turn into a living brass idol—
Now in front of you
    you yourself are the biggest problem

(Translation of "Nee Mundu Nuvve")

THE END OF THE THREAD

There are no new poems
Will the old poems work
Will the old poems
ring new
must ring
the poem within a poem does not die

The poems of well-known poets
the poems of unknown poets
all stand like penguins
on the sea shore
From afar
    colonies and colonies
    look like a single bird
Perhaps poems are just like that
All poems will merge into
                a single poem
If we can find the end of the main thread
    we can separate everything
    the world will appear crystal clear

(Translation of "Daaram Kosa")

THIS DAY THIS WAY

Let me welcome this day this way
        with a tea cup
        with a cigarette—
Each day in its own way is unique
Nobody knows what lies in its womb
        This day itself is time
        This day itself is time's limit
A flow that has no banks no end
To hold it in a fist
To puncture it with a needle
Don't know if it's impure or pure
Don't know if it's alive or not
Wrap it
as you would wrap a handkerchief around your wrist
The honey bee
that keeps flitting today
the lime that has ripened in the morning and fallen down today
Can I wrap my head with
the sacrifice of a life each day
a rebirth each day

(Translation of "Eerojunilaa")

THE JOURNEY HAS BEGUN

The journey has begun
When the journey began—it was one
now—many
        countless—all becoming one
An effort to see if poetry will help separate them
Maybe it's like counting the stars
as you keep counting you lose count
start counting once again
Where are you—amidst calculations that have no beginning or end—
caught amidst which eyelids—
We need a path
If we get hold of the tail of the path
        to pull it entirely
It will slip off can't grasp it
Finally to some childhood days
or the borders of youth
or to the vicinity of old age
like separating soaked gogulu—but
you can't bring anything together
Looks as if the doors are closed
as if everything is out in the open—but
walls keep springing up time and again
rooms come up

how will you break down invisible walls
how will you bring life to some conclusion
Something will remain intangible and
    keep haunting
as if all that is learnt
has been a waste
as if you have not seen what you ought to have seen
as if you have not learnt what you ought to have learnt
In the journey that begins time and again
there may be stopovers
but no end
Tear drops will fall and break
beneath the feet

(Translation of "Prayaanam Modalayindi")

IT HAS DAWNED

At last it has dawned!
        In the expansive universe
        one night has been spent
"It has dawned no need to fear"
        someone said
Isn't it a shadow that the night hounds
        where will it go
It's like when you open one door
closing another door
Someone is cutting you up
        as day and night
Can you escape life that's
                                hounding you
Everything lives
        with its opposing nature
When you really don't know yourself
                                anyone can oppose you
To which branch will you fix the swing and rock
Days will drop off without your knowledge
There's no time to pick it up like gleanings of a crop
Without your knowledge you will go around something
You won't be able to find the centre of gravity, your
                                        legs can't touch the ground

You will drink water and get suffocated
Someone will hold you by your hair and pull you out
The fear will not vanish even after reaching the shore
Who is folding you into a thin tracing paper that doesn't tear
You can't breathe
with all kinds of stupid fears in the head
searching for sentences, words
Door won't open
A frightening trench around life
Fiery boulders will keep rolling from above
A sound in sleep and in a dream
Someone is collecting water from a tank
The sound of all the trees all the crops all the birds
smiling gleefully heartily

(Translation of "Thellavaarindi")

NOTHING STOPS

Nothing stops
Everything moves
From its place to another place
the living being, the non living being too—
everything is in motion
Perhaps death means only motionlessness—
In this earthly world
    motion alone is beautiful
To view life means
only to catch hold of
    the one in motion in its entire vitality—
To live means
only to attain
    the very fruition of the character of evolution
Look at the farmer's hand
Does it seem so hard so rough
How many eras of conversation it would have had with mud
Isn't that the hand that moulded history
Perhaps it is because of this that one makes morsels
not just of rice but of mud
How can you experience the rebirth that I feel
when my father rubbed my back
with his hard hand

except when your mother
    took your cheeks to caress them

He comes to sit next to you and says
    "Move a bit"
You will move an inch
He will sit down leaning against you
In a little while he is you, you are him
What is there
    The journey
is for you just to become yourself

(Translation of "Edee Aagadu")

BIRDS DIE

No one is visible
but they will pierce with knives
will poke with needles
will tear the skin
No one is visible
They are burning us up even when alive
they are frying us like they fry a hen
cutting us into tiny tiny pieces
they are frying us on the skillet
they will dry us on the string
No one is visible
Not a squeak will be heard from the throat
They will cast a net and throw grains
they will break the wings and put them in the sling bag
they will slice the fingers, they will pull out the eyes

Nothing is visible
    Eyes filled with dust
Don't know if the route is new or old
An unknown feeling pours down like rain
The fields dry up for no reason
Birds die

(Translation of "Pakshulu Chanipothaayi")

STONE GODDESS

Nothing will be smooth
Nothing will happen smoothly
As you are walking on an even road
it caves in all of a sudden
        it becomes a deep pit
when you think it is all right
        accidents happen
a dark eye guards you all the time
you pull out your two hands from your two pockets—
        they are stubs
The body that was like a tender plant till some time ago
becomes dry and bare, no, becomes a cracked earth
A word will vanish before it is put on paper
Paths everywhere get closed
Dumb nights cry in silence
Nothing remains stable, will not be peaceful
Mirrors don't reflect your face
        they reflect skulls
from the eyes of the skull snakes will slither out
In the air fear swells and flows
Even in 2018 man is not healthy, has no protection
Nothing would be delicate and smooth
In the midst of the flow of lava on the road

rock gardens will be moving
Nothing is what it is
There is no place for a wild animal here
Here an exhibition of skulls
The sky will rain snakes
The link between forgetfulness and memory
          gets snapped, everything is topsy-turvy
Which tree will respond, which flower will blossom
A stone goddess will walk right through the village.

(Translation of "Raathi Devatha")

BETWEEN BODIES

How will you understand
        this hell-like state within the body
unless you yourself
        are in such a hell-like state
Is it one hell or two hells
three four five six hells
an assemblage of pooled up hells

Just as several animals exist in one animal
in one hell
experiences of several hells

Talking about it is difficult
To restore to life
        a dream broken into two
To restore is extremely difficult

(Translation of "Dehaanthara")

TO THE SKY BRANCH

Though I am hanging from the sky branch
don't know when I will fall down, where I will fall down
Didn't I come to rock
on the eye-like sky
Didn't I wish to see the entire universe swing
If the expansive universe is an eye ball
if the swelling water drop is an ocean
for the fellow who swings in the sky
sun, moon, clouds, stars
all are a fantastic colourful picture
Anyone may ask how can one swing
        without touching one's feet on the ground
        may be surprised—
Swinging in the sky feels the same as
walking on the ploughed field, in the mud
When in a state you don't know where to place your feet
swinging is the only option
Hanging holding the edge of
the sky that's like drenched black soil
is it like putting down on paper
the picture moving in your eyes
Where is the poetry that is confounding
It's like

each one turning oneself inside out and wearing it
It's there, the word is somewhere there
Is it the struggling uncertainty
of the cut earthworm
while turning over the earth with a spade!
Will I lose my hold, slip and fall
If I fall, in the middle of which word will I fall
A cloud will thunder
An eye will move
If I who have come like a kite near the clouds
fall
like a tamarind fruit
when some boy annoyed
hits it with a stone
I will have to turn into a scythe of the farmer

Maybe it's the farmer who had in fact
hung me on a hanger from the clouds

Now there's no difference
between the ploughed field and the sky
Swinging, swinging
I will fall on the horns of a bullock
or on rice flower

(Translation of "Aakaasam Kommaki")

THIS AEROPLANE

This aeroplane will never land
it will keep circling around like a bird
whether it has forgotten that there is the earth beneath
or mistook the sky for the earth
If you keep flying like this, crazy one,
where will you build your nest
where will you lay your eggs—
Isn't the earth or a tree that comes out from the earth
        necessary
Will you lay an egg
        in the nest of the gigantic sky
Do you want god Brahma to come and brood over it

No
Come down to the earth
Let's build our own nest
Let's cook our own food

(Translation of "Ee Vimaanam")

THE WHEEL OF RECOLLECTION

Rickshaw, car, bus
  they move, don't they
Moving on and on, they stop, don't they
They don't appear lifeless
As if they are breathing, are living
they move on beautifully
They have form have sight
a heart that entwines the body
How much of life have they seen
How many stories have they heard
Something always beats in their hearts
as if the bell in the temple is chiming
There is courage, there is companionship
They know
how to talk as they walk to sing as they walk
They throb with vitality
They lose themselves
  as if they are fully drunk
Their world in our world
our world in their world
  get woven
They entwine fingers with fingers
  and mock

Saying "Stupid fellow!"
    they laugh at me

The wheel of recollection keeps turning
The life lives on

(Translation of "Smriti Chakram")

NEEM TREE

Once upon a time
        we had a neem tree in our backward
Its trunk was bent
        and seemed like the beam of a palanquin
        also like a camel's neck
Sitting on the camel's neck
        going about we used to see the world
Singing "ohom, ohom"
we used to parade the princess
There were no hooked sticks
        either to stop or to take rest
All a procession
The thorns and stones under the feet—all only flowers
Who cared about time
Who cared about hunger or tiresomeness
To have led a carefree life was enjoyable

To climb a neem tree and swing
was pleasure to children in the village
In the nights, during sleep too
the tree would sing "ohom, ohom"

It used to
swing the body with sleep
Nobody would come and disturb
would spoil the quiet bliss

The pleasant breeze from the fields
would come and settle on us like a bird
Be it backyard, house, cattle or human beings
they would be hypnotized
If you take a pebble from your pocket
        and fling it into the sky
it will turn over several times, fall on the water in the lake
and frog leap like a flat tile

Don't know now
all those are surrounding me
like groundnuts roasted in the sand
with a sweet smell arousing hunger
They are enlivening this wretched moment
me too

The neem tree of those days
still puts its hands inside me
        stirs me

A stone that is not dead
will pass on from me to my grandson

(Translation of "Vepachettu")

BUILD A PLACE

Haven't you got used to it
even after so many days
even after seeing so many things
haven't you got used to it
        Are you still alive
Even after experiencing
so many difficulties, so many joys
so many sorrows, so many betrayals
so many hells, so many heartburns
hasn't it been doused—is the fire still there

Amazing
You should have been dead long ago
Should have turned into a corpse
Even after turning habit into food
after getting habituated to it too
where are responses
where are kindnesses
where are affections
Having become habituated to habit
you are a thing
a narcotic drug
a kerchief that's worn out

Everybody has to get used to it
Everybody has to die
*
Build a place
such as
a jungle where no ant can enter
a dark forest no crow can enter

(Translation of "Oka Sthalaanni")

I HEAR THE HUMAN BEING

A moment's despair
The very next moment hope, great hope
Hope as huge as a great struggle
I hear
sounds of the bangles in the morning
hear sounds of flowers
hear ripples moving in the lake
I hear
hear the earth
hear the sky
hear the sound of the earth's eye
that's slowly rotating
hear the tender sounds of tassels
at the end of the garment
worn last evening
I don't just hear the sounds
I see them keeping my eyes close to another's
see them thoroughly intensely
Strumming the strings somewhere deep below
I hear the resonance of the fingertips
Can't hear without seeing
can't see without hearing
        A despair

the very next moment hope as gigantic as life
I see
        the morrows
of the movement of heroes
who carry the weight of the struggles
I strum—strum the morning moments
I strum the strong resolves
of pigeons that perch on the eyes of the child
I look at the human being
hear the human being
who gets up early
carries huge hopes

(Translatiom of "Manishini Vintaanu")

THE POUNDING SONG

Hotel
even when there are so many people
even when there is so much of commotion—
that's aloneness for me
that's a Bodhi tree for me—
It cannot stir
    the inner world
Perhaps, it will move it closer
It won't douse the fire, it will light it
Hotel, bazaar, or house
    it's just a place, right
it's a place just like the chest, right—

Lanterns will light up
Flour will fall all around the mortar
The pounding song
    will echo in the clouds

(Translation of "Dampudu Paata")

ARROGANCE

One's arrogance
does not stop with him alone
    it will sting the next man
    it will look down upon him
Arrogance has no eyes
    it's a blind creature
It hangs upside down
    no love, no compassion
    no nature to embrace all
No self-knowledge
It is born out of blind belief
Arrogance has vengeance, has a hood
it has a tongue that spews fire
It neither reads itself
nor does it read the world
It is a disfigured power that
    moves about covering itself with night all the time
It's a horrifying form
It grows like water hyacinth
by morning it takes over the entire body
It's a constant drizzle
it showers thick and black

Who can slice it
    with an axe
except he himself

(Translation of "Ahankaaram")

DOGS

Barking
    is their nature
Worlds that are not visible to us, dangers too
        are visible to them
They keep awake
They wake us up
    Disturbance of sleep—
True, their aim is
    to disturb sleep, their duty

In an ungrateful world
they are the grateful ones

The poems they write
how wonderful it would be if we could read them

(Translation of "Kukkalu")

THE RAW DATURA FRUIT

During childhood
when you tossed a raw datura fruit, tightened your fist
turned it around and kept it underneath—
when the thorny mace-like raw fruit fell
tiny blood stains
        all over the other side of the palm—
when you shook it each touched the other
with the entire hand appearing blood-smeared—
painful though that was a childhood pleasure

What's it now
when invisible raw datura fruits
        prick the entire body—
somewhere something moves, breaks
like a thin streak spreading internally—
All of a sudden a murder of crows
        set off from the treetops
singing some tune
they fly out in all directions
The poem-puppy with the broken leg can't stir out
The two eyes
two red datura fruits
The raw datura fruit, the fist
the crow, the puppy me

(Translation of Ummeththa Kaaya")

IF HUMAN BEINGS WERE TREES

Head full of leaves
I haven't come walking under any tree
But, head full of leaves
Head like leaf-feathers—
Lush green aroma spreading all around the room
as if colourful baskets are made
on the banks of Musi river—
Maybe there is a tree inside the human being
Maybe that has sprouted like this
        flowered like this—
The rustling of leaves is heard
When all the clouds caress my head and move
a vague feeling of the roots stirring somewhere inside
a feeling of the water flowing
It looks like
a flock of birds seem to be coming
Don't know if they will build nests

When I walk
it doesn't look as if a human being is walking
Feels like a tree is walking, walking
If human beings were trees
if trees were human beings
        how wonderful would it be
How lush green would the universe be
how brilliantly would the world shine

(Translation of "Manushulu Chettlayithe")

THE SENTENCE IS GREAT

A sentence that exudes love
        is great
A sentence that gushes out of righteous indignation
        is greater
A sentence that's filled to the brim
with anger, with "the quality of mercy" too
that swells up and flows is greater still
One thing from another
another from another, another
it extends like that
Growing like that it becomes the Meru mountain
Who can destroy a sentence
        filled with kindness
Researching and researching all my life—
haven't I found an old word
a word that's the root of all—
Are we discovering what's already discovered!
Someone is screaming from within
"Set aside everything
all theories and live—live fully"
All this is a hanging bridge
        won't stay at one place

(Translation of "Vaakyam Goppadi")

A FARMER IS INDEED A FARMER

He had dropped from heaven
He wished to climb to the sky as if it were a mountain
Not that he didn't know that he should fly to the sky
        not crawl to it—
No, because he didn't want to do anything in an ordinary way—
Thinking as to why one shouldn't crawl to something
                                                            that one should fly to
to experience the crawling experience—
Turning the sky vertically he crawled up
the sun and moon, the stars under his stomach
filling his pockets with this much of mud
to scatter on the sky—
to grant earthiness to the sky
to scatter seeds there too
to plant saplings—
his imagination—if sky were to become earth
earth become sky—
what's the big difference
The dwellers of the sky will slip down to the earth
the dwellers of the earth will crawl up to the sky
Wherever a human being exists he is human
has to ready the plough with bullocks, plough the field, scatter seeds
grow crops for all

Farmer is indeed a farmer—brought Nasik
        poured it in Mumbai
A mountainness to Mumbai, a wateriness
a movement, a coolness
gave it a hardness and enlivened it

(Translation of "Raithu Raithe")

PROTECTING ANYTHING

How difficult it is to protect anything
Be it a thing, a relationship
a trust—a belief
a wondrous experience
anything, difficult to protect
In the context of things breaking
        even before one touches them
how difficult to protect any value
How difficult it is to protect a movement
one has marvelously built up
putting one's life at stake, sacrificing everything
pooling up all of one's strength
Building alone is difficult, destroying is easy
There is life that is being built
gradually and strongly.
It is not that easy to dismantle it.

Even when it's cracking on one side
it keeps growing densely like a creeper on another side
To decimate comrades who have learnt this skill
        is impossible
You my Communist brother
a symbol of nature that widens in ever so new ways—

Standing in front of the ocean
        I salute you with folded hands
You are my ocean
You are my oceanic battle

(Translation of "Dennayinaa")

WHAT FOR YOU

What for you my dear
If it's sunny you grow wings
If it rains you sprout
Entire nature is yours
Yours is the eternal dark body of harvested crop
Who can stop you
You who merge everything within you
can be counted as a new creation—
Each drop of rain falls
Every drop of rain that falls enters your body
Every ray that is born becomes yours
Looking at you I am planting myself

Here in this dark cave
maybe no light will survive
maybe no waft of wind will peep in
We say that
but if we pull the screen aside
you creep in
Like the letters of the alphabet on a copper plate
you stand without being erased
You weave me in and make me merge with you
Don't know about tomorrow morning but

you pour life into me for this moment
Why twigs
for one who roams about with wings of imagination
I wonder where all this strength comes from
wonder who has infused such a long life
A desire to conquer myself and stand
Isn't a syllable born
from a desire from a world of penance—
There are no days or nights
No decaying, no rotting
That's it like outer space
wide expansive
it blossoms

(Translation of "Neekemi")

WHERE THERE IS NO DISTANCE

Don't stand at a distance
Don't move far far away
Don't keep anyone at a distance
The world of the eyes is very vast
It will give place to any number of people
It will keep extending, extending in an ever widening way
It will cling on to the heart like the fragrance of a flower
There's a poem on a bird's feather, read it
Educate the nights a bit
Some pleasant fragrance
        pervades the entire room
Word has the ability to link this distance
Don't stand at a distance, don't move far away
There's a stream by the forest
There's a kid that drinks water without fear from the stream
Come! Take it into your hands
Look into its eyes—you will see
        hundreds of Buddhas
All nature will sing a song that augurs well
Isn't a single syllable enough
for you to see yourself—to hide yourself
Ask the lotus that keeps its hand under its chin
It will explicate the world little by little

The future will glide down a bit
        Hold your palm and drink
        You will find all as one
It will tell you
        that joy resides where there are no distances

(Translation of "Dooramleni Chota")

ALONG THE FOOTSTEP

A little bit of belief
At every step confidence—
That there is still a little left
that it will well up again like water
Which step
will fall on which globe
I do not know
even so taking a step putting a step forward—
Isn't it only forward—from the front yard
to the immense outer space—
Isn't just a step the foundation
for all of man's movement
Steps on steps
Walking without faltering, without falling off
For man's complete growth
    only this very step
the step that is all powerful
the step that has filled itself with the power of imagination
The steps are being taken
What step is this
Not defeated not receding
determined footsteps of many before me
Reading the steps

reciting the steps
I putting
step after step
Look tomorrow morning
I will go so far that you can't reach
Right behind me
my poet-river will follow me

(Translation of "Adugu Venta")

STANDING IN FRONT OF THE HOUSE

Who could it be
that's crying in front of the house
I can even hear the sobs
When I get up open the door and see
no one is there—darkness
is slithering away like a snake
Even when I come back sit and close my eyes
I distinctly hear the sobbing
Who could it be?
My ears are keenly watching the sobbing

Even sound can see
I touch the sorrow
in front of the house
Touch can hear, can see
Night becomes a river of sorrow
A sob that can be heard in sleep too
A forest that is smouldering within

Someone is crying endlessly

(Translation of "Inti Mundu Nunchoni")

OUTSIDE THE GATE

Outside the gate next to the footpath
he placed a chair and sat in the sun
The sun in the winter he thought would be a little warmer
    and pleasant
From the top leaves like tamarind leaves were falling
Each time the wind blew, they were raining like a shower
He compared himself with the falling leaves
Leaves like the bottu on a young woman's forehead
were falling gracefully over him now and then

He couldn't accept that he was like the leaves
for he had all the powers alive in him still
for he was the symbol of all nature—
Leaves might fall from the top flowers might fall
raindrops like flowers might fall
but that he shone, that from the time the sapling was planted
up to its becoming a gigantic tree covering the entire sky he alone
Now
he might have been trapped in this situation
Somewhere on the banks
water might have forced its way, forced its way and come out
might create an imposing watery gateway
There a cultivable land might blossom

like a poem
It might pull the sky towards it
A yearning to hold his head high even when severed
only a desire to turn the universe on the finger
        like a top
Not to yield is a human trait
He who sat beneath the tree
        kept watching the leaves fall
        kept watching the wind blow
He was watching human beings
        eager to fight battles move like that
What does it matter where he was—
He was a human being, a human being
        growing to a massive stature

(Translation of "Getu Bayata")

WITH ONE PERSON NOT BEING THERE

So much emptiness
with just one person not being there!
House empty body empty heart empty
all the surroundings empty empty—
Amazing
So empty so bare as if it's lifeless
        if just one person is not there—
How he occupied the whole house
how he controlled everyone under one soul
how he endowed a movement to everything
how he provided oxygen that's life's necessity
how amazing surprising
like the sand on the lake bank where water keeps
                                        oozing as you dig
like the water bird that moves about wet
I think he is only one
perhaps not one
perhaps several people
who stimulate
everyone's childhood
        with bubbling energy—
maybe it's my illusion to think it is one person—
Maybe he is the yogi

who pushes me into my childhood pulls me out from there
plants me here and there—in a garden
        in an orchard in a dense forest—
Are the ones we see real—maybe he is the magician
who makes us see a life that is invisible—

Wherever he may be he will be just like that
That he is not one can be felt only when he is not there
The one who had filled within his body
coconut groves mango groves banana plantations
streams rivulets rivers
the live spirit that establishes us as we are
in his presence
we see our own selves

(Translation of "Okkadu Lekapothe")

AWAY FROM EVERYTHING

Away from everything
like a train that has stopped at the station since god knows when—
Legs are getting rusted
Not being able to move is death
Eyes are turning into motionless darkness
Where's the way, doesn't move backward
        doesn't move forward too
At the place it has stopped, it stops right at that place
        gets destroyed
A gusty wind
zips through from this side to that side
Its horrendous sound reverberates in its own ears
It's like a tree where no bird sits
Maybe it's gone crazy
it stands like an extinguished lamp

No one will call it back
No one will call it to come forward
It stands like a deaf person

(Translation of "Annintikee Doorangaa")

NEAR THE PATIENT

What smell will one find near a patient
One will find the smell of a disease
One will find the smell of deteriorating health
        Ill health will pour down even from the sky
        It will spread like moisture in the surrounding air
Perhaps seeing this room they would have created hell
Where does a person's ill health come from
Is his ill health just his own
Perhaps not—
Perhaps it's the consequence
of several pollutions
societies histories and atrocities that have no atonement—
There's tomorrow but can one see it
        hear it even as a faint outline
Perhaps it's the ocean of the immoral essences
familial legacies environments—
Where does he have the energy
        to open the window of the east and see
Don't beg meanly
infallible porticos of weakness and helplessness
        that drain your life spirit
Some invisible pleas
will envelop like dense clouds

Inside that person
who sits holding his hand too
the shadow of despondency will linger on
Will anyone be able to break
the glass bottle of such an atmosphere
Where's the source of these sorrows
the vision of life—
Why has this life turned out to be so horrible
I asked all the poets of the world to respond
Everyone brought in their poems and placed them before me
with their vacant faces
All mere descriptions, mere commentaries—
That experience alone is stable
Eternal—the origin of everything
"*The more you confine me*
The more I will spill over"
Sukirtharani

(Translation of "Rogi Daggara")

THE SENTENCE OF THE WATER BIRDS

Conversation
        with another poet
on a winter morning—
The excavations of Harappa and Mohenjo-daro
the broken pots tell a history
Morning's conversation is like the first coffee
It fills some warmth and some wakefulness
The dormant energy wakes up and opens its hood like a snake
        The conversation
from Kunwar Narayan[8] to Golconda
from Golconda to Darwish
from Darwish to Ibrahim Nirgun
        become much more animated
Through the living history in words of
Kilamanur Madhu's pneumonia poem
Desa Mangalam's "Curfew" relive again
Seamus Heaney, Metta Nageswara Rao,
Dr. Mutyam, Subbarao Panigrahi—all get mixed up
get mixed up in this morning, move away
This morning is a conversation between the past and the present
They lay roads inside me
from Parvatipuram to Padmanabha of Thiruvananthapuram

---

8 Kunwar Narayan and others mentioned are progressive writers and activists.

It walks a few steps peacefully
over the city of internal turmoil
On a morning like this
some naughty boy will hurl a stone
It will quickly take a dip in the lake and go round in circles

This morning will speak
It will move away weaving a sentence of tiny water birds

(Translation of "Neetipittala Vaakyam")

POEMS

Poems
sleep in my bed
They put their legs on my belly
embrace my neck and lie down
They make a hue and cry pestering me to narrate stories
Not Ramayanam or Bharatam
I believe I must narrate the stories of gandabherunda[9] birds
"Each gandabherunda bird
is as big as our house" I say
Their wings encompass the whole sky
Gandabherunda birds attack
the kingdom
Like eagles carrying away chicken
they carry away human beings and eat them up
The population of the country will decrease
They had carried away the army and ate it up
For the one who destroys the gandabherunda birds
and rescues the people
he said he would give his daughter's hand in marriage
and hand over the kingdom
Lakhs and lakhs of gandabherunda birds
are hovering around

9 Mythical bird of a huge size with two heads

A farmer who came from the village
    stood in front of them shook his upper cloth
blew with his mouth
as if shelling thousands of fire arms
Fire swarmed destroying them
The country became prosperous
The small farmer as usual as if nothing had happened
putting the upper cloth on his shoulder
    went to the field to work
The poem that had placed its legs on my belly
got up
    looked me up and down
then went back into itself

(Translation of "Padyaalu")

MUST BE EXPRESSED ELOQUENTLY

Some things must be expressed eloquently
Some things must be held back at the throat
Some things must be held back
by holding one's breath at the bottom of the lake
Some must be hidden deep inside
with an expression of a poignant smile
Who will tell you all these
It's your life that will tell you
It teaches you to walk on the wire
        with a single leg
All around there is this much of the world
these many people
Will anyone be able to bandage your wound
be able to make you who have collapsed stand up
You keep floating in the air
        without any support
Except for the sky above
        no earth can be seen below
In the middle of the ocean
floating in the sky without any support
whose finger will you hold on to
Only when you stand firmly
        will everything gather around you

will kiss you with the nose
Some things must be stopped
        right at the navel
Shouldn't cross the lips
Shouldn't be broadcast
to the world
Keep storing up
everything
The water will flow in a thin streak
Plants will sprout gradually

(Translation of "Uggabattali")

TWO LINES

Write two lines
Two lines per day
The holy stanzas/steps of two feet
Two feet that encompass all literature
        all music
will be eternally reverberating
The two feet/lines that have taken in the secret of
        the universal beauty
the beat that is produced when earth rotates
cradle song bedtime song shaped or
without shape—this is a musical cycle
Grease around its axle
turns inside softly smoothly
A sweet needle that stitches together nights and days—

Only two lines—write let's see
How will you write without anything
The words that form in an orderly manner
know not anarchy
A mode a process alone is their body
Get up sometime around five, close your eyes
        imagine two lines
        dream two lines—

Entire water bodies
will move in your words with a gurgling sound
Some living sound will swell up high
I don't know what auspicious moment it is
It's a moment when the entire universe will come alive once again
so one can rub one's eyes—
        get ready to witness a beauty
A flower
        will quietly bloom
All the halls of prayer around the world will
        open up

A woman will just like that get into the lake
fill a potful of water and come up.

(Translation of "Rendu Paadaalu")

THE LOVER IS EARTH

I hid secretly
in the layers of the earth
    How would you know
except if you are in my place
Making you lie down on the bench
    as someone is cutting you up
asking you to enjoy—
I have been hiding
since many years, since thousands and thousands of years
incognito so as not to be exposed—
There's no asking
    if this is right or wrong
That's what had happened
That's what is happening
Are secret love
and secrecy one and the same thing—
Need to have the strength to dig
like sharpening the sickle
    reaping the harvested paddy
There must be one who reaps
There must be one
tying them in bundles
heaping them

Who will ask the earth
why have you hidden all these—
The lover is earth

(Translation of "Premikudoka Bhoomi")

A LEAF FALLS

A leaf falls
There
a sprout raises its head
Singing in a crore of voices
    it blossoms
They came with
knives daggers crowbars spades
They came
Laughing the tree
shed a few leaves
sprouts sprouts galore
sprouts the entire forest—
They spread out
becoming heroic tales

The forests will lay siege

(Translation of "Aaku Raaluthundi")

BEAUTY OF A STONE

The beauty of a stone is its own
The beauty of water is its own
Water in stone
Stone in water
Perhaps once in a way
stone becomes water water becomes stone
the roles they take on change
the thinginess alone keeps expanding
gets transformed
The fundamental truth is only one, isn't it?

Grandson picks up and brings all the stones he finds
Perhaps he finds something in the stone
that I can't find
When Anjaneya brought the stones
        Nila built the bridge
Bridge is a sentence
Nila is Anjaneya
Water stones that's a verb of action
A sentence with a verb of action is a movement

(Translation of "Raayi Soundaryam")

AS IF A PAGE HAD BEEN TURNED

Is a tune
        from meditation
Is meditation
        from a tune—don't know.
Perhaps both are the same
No tune without meditation
No meditation without a tune
The spindle keeps turning
The end of jute fibre keeps weaving
        from the hilltop
Arranging stones in a row
the creator terms it a very long collocation
The river that begins
        like a light hum
spreads across the entire outer space
like mother Ganga
All are only calls only shrieks
I apply oil, disentangle the hair
        weave a sentence
Someone shouted at the house corner
In sleep someone called out silently
Don't know if I responded or started to sing

It dawned
as if a page had been turned
I turned the other side
Started writing
        the second sentence

(Translation of "Pagee Thippinattu")

YOU WRITE A POEM

You write a poem
That flies
How can I enter your poem that flies
except with wings of imagination—
If you write half the poem
I have to complete the second half
Every poem is incomplete
I have to complete it
    Whatever anyone gives is just a half
    we have to fill in the second half
You pick up a word there a word here
and build a nest
Must lay an egg only in that
When someone some people for many days some days
brood over it it becomes a young one
Becoming a young one
it begins to sing

(Translation of "Nuvvoka")

TO IMAGINATION

I am fixing fingers on imagination
    I am attaching feet on to it
I am giving a voice of a tone of protest
I am teaching it
    the nature to weave itself as it feels like
For a man hanging from nothingness
    nothingness is the earth
The background for imagination is the earth itself
Its fingers are rooted in the earth
    that keeps rotating
You cannot count the fingers
    that imagination has
As many wings as it unfolds
that much does it roll in the dust
    In truth it is a living being—
Knows if you pinch the cheeks
Does not ask for a generous donation
It hangs on to a tear drop that falls from somewhere
and slides down
over the cheeks, or the chest—
There would be someone there
A person who is like a seed
    that gives breath to the earth

It lives for that man
Is there anywhere anytime
where imagination does not grow?

It gives and giving pleases
nightness for nights
morningness for mornings
humanness for humans

(Translation of "Oohaki")

TO THE SUN

"Switch on the light"
There should be no darkness in a house where people live
There should be no kind of darkness surrounding me
Even if it is a great darkness
I don't want it
Isn't it for this much of light
that the sun gets on to a seven horsed chariot
and roams about
Who will pay salary to the sun?

(Translation of "Sooryudiki")

HOW LONG LIKE THIS

How long like this
        on one leg with one wheel
        with a carriage without the horse—
What's this useless battle—?

Whether useful or useless
can't say now

Only the battle will be there
        that's eternal
Fighting the battle alone
        is life's mission

Nothing can be solved in a moment
Regardless of
        profit or loss
the farmer will go on cultivating

He will keep pulling the transporting boat
to the canal's end

(Translation of "Enthakaalamilaa")

THE SHED

What the hell
how much they love human beings
When you go near them to feed green grass
they lick your hands and face to their heart's fill
The slightly rough tongue
seems to be reading a language unfamiliar to us
the body gets sudden goose pimples
They eat grass they drink overnight gruel
If you throw jute stalk they enjoy
chewing with closed eyes
If you scrub the entire body with hay
the moisture in their eyes will caress you

It will say something you will hear
You caress its body with love

For a while you will become its calf
For a while more it will become your mother
That's why
the shed will be
        so wonderful
House
or shed love is important isn't it?

(Translation of "Chavidi")

THE KNOT

All music is
    in this knot ayya—
A knot that
    a small child had tied to this string—
Don't know what mantras he recited and tied this knot—
Even if the flower hanging from the knot falls down
    the knot will still remain
Of how many knots is this life
As we untie the knots
there arise many more knots
Knot does not mean an ordinary knot
It's a knot that a Brahma-like child has tied
don't know how many secrets of creation he has filled
    tying this knot—
Perhaps he has hung the globe around my neck
    in the form of this knot—
No bad omen will befall me
No harm will come to me—
Will you believe the knot
Will you believe the mantra
I don't believe the knot nor do I believe the mantra
but I believe the boy
I believe the boy

who is the incarnation of the future
Boy does not mean a boy
The boy who imprisoned all the three periods of time
    and tied the tricky knot
A boy like the Trinity
    In every house
    there must be a boy like this

(Translation of "Mudi")

GETTING UP

Getting up, we come into the world
Then living begins
The body that had been death-like till then
    will open up with movements
Casting the net begins
casting the net, pulling it out—
There will be a hole between
    freshness and serenity
Weeping begins—
From the plant to a huge tree
from the insect to the bird—
    can't understand anything
Opening the eyes wide
looking sharply at
the sky and the earth the mother and the child begins
No objection nothing is untouchable
Pulling all pulling each thing in

You drink tea
You light a cigarette
You give biscuits to the puppies
They sing songs unknown to us
You close the fist open it and look

You notice that the letters of the alphabet are growing there
Don't know who scattered the seeds
The plants grow and salute the sun

You set out determined
not to destroy anything

Some boy has started to write
a, aas[10] on the slate

(Translation of "Lechi")

10 A and aa refer to the first two letters of the Telugu alphabet.

NOW

Now
who will ask you "How are you?"
neither do they have the time nor patience—
Each one is looking forward
to someone asking about his welfare—
A pitiful condition has come about
as if everything is dead
as if one is living in vacant stone-cities
        as if no one is moving about
as if a sand storm is blowing in the desert
as if the already dead are dying
as if the limbs are falling off right there

You want tender greetings
        caring looks
want kind date trees
How do you think people will wander around
a terrain where anthills sprout
This is a serpent garden—there's no scope for friendship here
No resurfacing of the past no past memories

Only absolute death
Only absolute death

(Translation of "Ippudu")

AS THOUGH CLIMBING STEPS

As though climbing steps
he keeps climbing up dangers
For the onlookers
dangers seem like jubilation perhaps—
He internalizing everything
The weapons are not external, only internal—
How will one know the secret of life
Only in living the life—
He never thought never wrote it down
that it should continue like this
that it will continue like this
He believed that experiencing what he liked alone is
        the truth
What will remain in the end
        life will remain
        experience will remain
What shines till the end is
        nothing but experience
Believing that experience alone is joyful
he keeps riding the cart
        moves along
Who is that—
It could be anyone

(Translation of "Metlekkinattu")

FOOD

"Who needs a beauty parlour
        it's food that one needs"
How beautiful is food
Food that gives life to the living
Food that fills all the essence of beauty
Food that goes
beyond the lips beyond the boundary walls of the teeth
right inside forces its way into the tunnel
moves in twists and turns like a snake
flows to a distance of a thousand yojanas[11] and transforms into energy
Food that gives tastes of all kind
as it dances unrestrained throughout the universe
while the anklet bells of the dry thumma fruit tied to
                                        its leg resound
When a stainless Taj Mahal of a silver morsel is
flung into my stomach-ocean
all beautiful things float just like that on the waves
caress me and break open like bubbles
        The one who eats the morsel
        hears the sound of the bursting of the bubble
All the primeval imaginings arise only from there

---

11 Yojana refers to a distance of about eight to nine miles

I alight a boat and go to the moon
Revolving around the moon
        I call out to Lord Vishnu
O Universal One, O Lord Vishnu
O Kasi Annapoorna
The entire beauty of the
Universe becomes mine

(Translation of "Buvva")

WORKING

Working hands are wonderful
Speaking mouth is wonderful
What kind of life is it
        without work without speech—
All civilizations cultures
        only around work around speech—
All wars all revolts
        only for the liberation from exploitation of labour
only for speech without repression—
Work itself is beauty, speech itself is beauty
Trying to remember trying to remember
Remembering again remembering yet again
        I discover a word
Word is a symbol of the progress of the entire human race—
The sky beckons
the earth answers
The sky and the earth meet in one and the same word
The sky and the earth
meet in one and the same human being
Man who possesses work in one hand word in another hand
        is invincible
        is the architect of the world-order
Look at the hands of Vanajamma who makes tea

Look at the eyes of Venkamma who sweeps the streets
The entire creation like pigeons
        merges with them
The truth and Sivudu stand on either side
gather everything
        internalize them

(Translation of "Panichese")

WHEN

Will poetry move
if you sit without moving in one place
Will it move
    when you move without respite
Will it move in the sun, will it move in the rain—
Will it move
    when you pluck each cloud and are putting it in your pocket
Will it move
when you are climbing down a hill or climbing up a hill
Will it move
when parents outside are worried as children are writing
                                                their exams inside
Is there an auspicious moment a place a time
when a stranger comes and stands in the front yard
when two leaves fall
when two flowers bloom
when a born blind person
    is searching for the way with a stick—
will it move sometime?
Difficult to say
when it will move
when it will speak—
When it will break and fall on you
it is difficult to say—

(Translation of "Eppudu")

CAN'T MOVE ANYWHERE

Can't move anywhere
What's greater than
getting up in the morning and writing four poetic sentences
I think it's a good beginning for this day
Who can say
how any day will begin
When everything is being swept away in the flow of time
what's the meaning of the word eternal
I think it's good
to look at everything at that very moment
There's past it's over
There's future it's not visible
The creature that is caught between the two is man
Listening to the song of the bee trying to become a bee
Perhaps writing four sentences in the morning
is like that too

(Translation of "Etoo Kadallenu")

AEROPLANE

Taxiing taxiing
        the aeroplane suddenly takes off
becomes a snake-bird
With the invisible wings sprouting
        it joyrides in the sky
I call this a word
call it vapour of imagination
        that simmers keeps simmering
Broadly speaking I am in there not there
This is nothing but metal a metal that is fickle
It's like when it's drizzling
putting the grass for the buffalo
everything being soggy wet green and tender—
It's like running running
jumping nude into the lake
This is a streak of grass delightful
It's like the sun setting on the back of the head
of someone who is returning from the farm
This sets
rising in front of your eyes moving to the back of your eyes
Just as a spark of a fire is born
when you keep cotton and strike firestones
Will the distinction between an irrigation canal and a sewage canal

be erased or grow bigger?
In a condition where everything is getting merged
that one cannot differentiate
will the cotton cob break open into a white hue
Will uthareni[12] plant make its appearance
        in the fence between houses

Will ask Kedarnath Singh[13]
with his legs in the village
        and head in the city
(Translation of "Vimanam")

---

12 Uthareni refers to prickly chaff flower.
13 Kedarnath Singh is a well-known Hindi poet.

THE FIRST TIME

Nowadays it feels
like writing for the first time like conceiving for the first time—
The sweet pains of strong embraces that seem to nearly suffocate
in the ecstasy of the first intercourse
Like one is pregnant after ten years—
Everything fresh
All these words fresh all these imaginings fresh
Like migrant birds perching ever so freshly
I am not able to make out which is my word which not mine
Not really the first time but the first time—
Covering the nights with a blanket
like someone calling from inside from inside the womb—
Like a plant sprouting all of a sudden growing
becoming a gigantic tree—everything fresh
Not as if it's an alien land—it's as if
I discovered this land right now—stepped on it
As if it has slipped away from the grasp
As if a huge gulf has formed
between me and my sentence—caught in the grip
slipping away from the grasp—
Years haven't gone by
decades centuries haven't gone by—
As if stepping on a threshold that's not mine—

So much change so soon
Even when I'm in front of me—as if it's not me
This distant pain of being another—
becoming so severe as if swirling and getting drowned—
Perhaps
the wordlessness that has formed
between one who has stopped and one who is continuing to walk—
This is not normal
        it pulls pulls deep inside
till you die—
A poetic line
        that's being swept away in the water slope

(Translation of "Tholisaari")

WATER BIRD

He thought
    it was difficult to
        retain a zest for life
That it would also be difficult to
    retain the sword without losing its sharpness
That it would also be difficult to
    save a single petalled banti[14] flower or a thousand petalled lotus—
That it would also be difficult to
comb the wings of the river that goes around this hill and flies
Don't we have to plant the trees
that have sprouted in the sky
Don't we have to hide the smile that has opened up on the earth's lip
in the shores of the sky-lake
How can the rainbow that lives as if it has no parts
though it has all of them
        tightly embrace man
How can it make him eternal
in the entire universe?
From where can one get
        the most powerful the life-giving water—
That's true—
It is indeed difficult to make this small light—this life eternal

14 Banti refers to marigold.

It's not easy to get prepared for a long drawn out battle
    that one has never heard or seen before
What shall we learn from
        the bird that walks effortlessly on water
We must catch hold of
some secret magical principle from
    the primeval man who is walking steadily along
                                            the crumbling mountain cliff
We must imbibe
some plunging and rising trait
of a water bird that is drowning in water and rising up

(Translation of "Neetipitta")

TIME MEANS

Time means nothing but exact time
At five means exactly at five
        not a moment more
        not a moment less
Five means exactly five—
A single moment is vital in the universe
Planets may change their course
        all disorder
Time cuts you to your size
Time is a great tailor
You can't roll in bed
                in a relaxed lazy manner
You have to get up quickly set everything in order
The world moves according to a beat
This is the music of the universe
Can't take one sangathi[15] more
one sangathi less
an orderly way—beautiful
        perhaps life
Nothing stops that will continue to move
Step after step you too have to move
The wakeful sun waking up everything

15 Sangathi refers to variation in a song.

brings them to life
Breathe in these soft sunrises as life breath
The whole outer space will thrive in you

A certain time means a certain time
Time means exact time
Five means exactly five

(Translation of "Time Ante")

LONELINESS

How constricted has loneliness become
        the attack of memories has increased
The attack of memories of childhood has increased all the more
        Feel suffocated
Perhaps it is wrong to think of loneliness as being alone
Who is the boy under the thumma tree in summer
who is gathering dry thumma fruits
Who is the boy who is gathering shells along the canal
Herds and herds of cattle raising dust
shaking their heads—coming towards the lake
Who is the one smoking a chutta with the upper cloth
                                        beneath his buttocks
under either a date palm tree or a palm tree
Why is the stream quivering like a water pot
There is an attack from all sides
on me who is sitting alone
Placing my hand against my eyes I am looking up keenly
Who are coming in groups and groups?
        Birds or human beings?
At a time when I am extending myself
        as hundreds and thousands
One is not just one
        perhaps not alone
Just as no note exists by itself, no human being exists alone

(Translation of "Ontarithanam")

NORMALLY

Normally
    the spring door in front
        has no value
There's no need to really notice it either
    But a friend has said he is coming
    Looking forward, looking towards the door—I
Every time it moves
the one who leaves and the one who comes swing in the mirror
My look falls there rises up again
The normally valueless objects become significant
                                        depending on the situation
        become valuable
Caught in the spring door
time swings
on anticipation

(Translation of "Maamoolugaa Ayithe")

TO THE MOUTH, TO THE HAND

There's no meaning to the mouth to the hand
        You can look as you eat
        You can eat as you look
        To the little child
        who eats idli as he watches the TV
        his grandmother speaks thus
He does not have the power
to do two things at the same time
        without getting drowned in either
He can drown completely
and do only one thing
He can either keep looking
or he can keep eating
The happiness in being involved
we do not know
        as much as he does

(Translation of "Notiki Chethiki")

LIKE AN OLD POEM

Who's this who is hidden
        between the pages
                like an old poem?
Looks like an orphan
Looks like a dead poem

Is he too one of the many children in the country
who have become orphans even with their parents alive?
After many years
he is found in the pages of the book
He would be seven
A dried up face having cried endlessly
as if a shirt has been put
        on a skeleton
A restrained smile
        from intense shyness—
Who's this, who's this, I wonder
On looking carefully, seems to be exactly like me
If you look keenly into his eyes
all nations will compete
        to line up and stand
They are glowing in a pitiful face
two eyes that have hidden sparks of fire

(Translation of "Paatha Padyamlaa")

THE STORY OF A CERTAIN RAMU

"My wife scolding
or my granddaughter crying
or the TV blabbering like that"
they ought to be there—it's a daily routine
How much better
        will this life be
In this category of life
it's a kind of happiness sadness
There's no history without sounds
There's no life without sadness
These don't disturb me
They are catalysts stimulants background music
Who will understand except someone like me
Every day is a festival—danger too
There's no distinction here between festival and danger

What shall we expect
from this life from this society
other than to somehow pull on
other than to drag this boat
        up to the sleep-river

(Translation of "Oka Ramu Katha)

GOODBYE SAMBALPUR

Goodbye, Sambalpur, goodbye
Goodbye to Sambalpur University
Goodbye to "Mahanadi"
Good bye to the coal mines of Mahanadi
Good bye to Surya Swami
I am taking a tender leaf from you
I am taking the newly birthing
Suryanarayanamurthy
Taking the soul of Gangadhar Meher
the great poet who stands twirling his moustache
at the main entrance of the University
Wide stretches of land
I am taking an ancient culture
that's buried in the lands
the fighting legacy that's hidden
in the lives of the tribals
the coal mines

I next to you Odisha
I in your bed Odisha
You one hand I another hand
Shall we join the two hands—
Odisha! Odisha—

(Translation of "Selavu Sambalpur")

IN THE GLASS

In the glass
        you pour four drops of liquor
        some water shake and drink
There's the glass there's the liquor there's the water
You mix them and pour it down your throat
Is mixing up everything poetry
tying a knot of unity to things that are divergent!
You're there the world's there the life's there
Looking at all these tasting them experiencing them
you scream saying you have discovered something new
                Is that creativity?
Where nothing exists—something being made up
establishing its existence—is that poetry!
Everything will be distinct
When they are distinct they are nothing
All getting mixed a life is born
                That's poetry
At that moment the outcome of penance that sages attain
some unique bliss
spreads across like words
A burning stove by mistake
instead of a stick you put your finger
        Is that struggle the assemblage of sentences

You make a small pill pour life
on to a paper
It moves it walks around it dances
dances holding its breath
        and crosses a distance of yojanas

A rain drop falls
The world rotates rapidly on the palm
You don't realise where you are
But being like that is poetry

(Translation of "Glaasulo")

BABY

Mother or sister carries the baby
in the busy bazaar in the humid rain—
        How much of weight does she carry
                As much as the earth
As much as the weight of life
        the shaping of which one doesn't know
One day she too had ridden on someone else's shoulder
performed such a victorious journey—
        Where are the words
        To talk about a life
        that's spell-bound where are the words—
Remembrance of crying hoarse on the lake bund
remembrance of crying copiously
Somebody put a red pencil mark
on the places where blood had flown
        on the earth that's a great support—
No stopping ever at a single place
No drinking water leisurely
For this little devil
I am breaking open the ground here
breaking stones
I am legislating
that the dry trees must sprout that it should shine bright

with flowers and fruits
The voice of the one suffering
is the word that is cleansed
a word equal to a curse—

Mother or sister must carry the baby
Must kiss the baby
the earth too.

(Translation of "Pasibidda")

COPACABANA BEACH

A rag on the waist
Another rag on the breasts
The entire beach they—
Doesn't look like they have come from the city to the seashore

Looks like they have come crawling from the water
like crabs from the sea
They fill up the entire shore
No matter their age
lying on their back sunbathing
What a seashore is this
as if someone has scattered
human beings along the entire stretch—
Becoming one
with nature in nature—is bliss

How can seas without human beings
        be beautiful
Human being is but beautiful
Human being is but a sea

(Translation of "Copacabana Beach")

THE GODDESS OF REJECTION

Who is this Mona Lisa
She is only the fruition of the essence of the lands of Odisha
She is the recipient of the essence of the revolt of the adivasis
She is the wakeup call of the cock of backwardness
In a fistful of a person a mountain of courage daring—
It's great to oppose anything
The attack on the rooted beliefs
The body is indeed great
The body inside the body is even greater
Only a few are able to hold on to something tight in their fist
        and not let it slip
The unwavering soul in the wavering body
Only a few are able to hear the song of the soul
That is the first letter of the alphabet
        only to the nectar-like essence that has experienced suffering
From Kurda road to Bhuvaneswar
the Chilka lake that has woven
I am not an astrologer but
I want to look
over the past present and future
        I wish to see your journey
Is there a relationship between
you and the god of Puri Jagannadh

Are you the crescent moon of Chandrabhaga!
You are the primeval goddess
carrying the bow and quiver
        journeying on the forest track
You are the Mother Goddess who rules everyone
Filled in your poetry a language a culture
a rejection
Hanging a few strands of hair on your face
you who are roaming about without a care
are the Parvati who made the turmeric Vinayaka
You're the mother
    to poetry that cares for none
Get angry be happy
    bless the world
What is the relationship between
    the Mona Lisa of the past and you?

A fury behind the calm
A harshness in kindness

Long live Mona Lisa
writing a few poems
Live long
Long live Mona Lisa long live

(Translation of "Thiraskaara Devatha")

[Mona Lisa is a leading Odiya writer and poet. She and Shafi Shauq, along with me, visited Brazil.]

SMOKE PIPE

Sometime
in some village
a young boy sat
blowing at the fire with a smoke pipe—with a book on his lap
The soggy dung cakes of the rainy season
emit more smoke than fire
The smoke swarms the house
almost choking the boy
As tears roll down his eyes
when he looks at the world—
everything hazy like unclear screens—
After many years of screens, like a doll—
pulling out a dry palm leaf from the thatch
        thinking of cooking rice—
After so many years here now
there's no boy no hut no stove either
no smoke pipe to blow
but
there are eyes filled with tears

(Translation of "Pogagottam")

A PIECE OF GINGER

Don't know
when the wife
    put the piece of ginger in the earth—
As soon as it drizzled a bit
the ginger plant stood up
    lifting its hands wonderfully like that
Emitting yellow colour so much
it stood so beautifully so regally
        conversing with the wind—
It does not know it is medicine
        that it cures diseases
In its existence
    transforming into a huge tree
    transforming into a huge mountain—
It might not know
about the living and non-living beings
about violence about wickedness
neither is there a necessity to know
You might not know
that near the red light in the morning
    ginger turns to tasty murabba
You need not say
specifically about yourself

your personality its hues
Your meaningful existence tells it all
I lift my hands and salute
the ginger plant that stands up
lifting its hands wonderfully

(Translation of "Allam Mukka")

ONE SUMMER

In such
a scorching summer
from four dust tracks to the village lake
with no slippers on the feet with no cloth over the head
with a shirt hanging with no buttons—
how many places did he search
for the lost buffalo
When he came near the lake bund
the buffalo was not among the cattle in the lake—
Roaming around ways and dust tracks
when he came near the shed
right in front near its peg the lost buffalo
When the eyes were dropping tears
the lightning that shone on the lips was only the smile
The boy that was then wearing it and going about
is this old man now

Distances are not always filled with sorrow
They are not cruel summers
They are also half bloomed
    happy orchards

(Translation of "Okaanoka Yendaakaalam")

IN THIRUVANANTHAPURAM

Early in the morning in Thiruvananthapuram—
    an early morning walk—at five itself

I met Padmanabha on the way—
"O' Swami! How come so early in the morning!"
"What do you want me to do?—Your Telugu poets have come
and disturbed me. They woke me up."

"Our people are just like that. They don't sleep.
They don't let others sleep. Ours is a waking up race.
But you're Anantapadmanabhashayana[16] aren't you?—
What's your problem?"

"You think I sleep all the time.
No, being awake when asleep
    asleep when awake—
    I have worked hard at it.
There's not much of difference between wakefulness and sleep
Keeping awake all the time is an art
Poets know this art—ought to know
For poets without borders for poets between languages
deep sleep is only in name

16 Eternally sleeping Padmanabha

Poets ought to know to sit on a spear and do penance
Two faces to living one sleep two wakefulness
I don't sleep at night
I sleep within—within me I am a mind voyager
Why should you come to see me who is asleep
Poets ought to know
        how to move from one state to another—"

"Swami! Shall we have tea in that tea shop?"

"Let's go! Drinking tea in the morning is
    to drink the morning."

(Translation of "Thiruvanthapuramlo")

HOW SO

How this will end
    he too doesn't know
only to keep waiting—
Will this earth hit another planet
Will male and female not remain separate become one
If there is no night will the day alone remain
Will a time come when there are no wicked people
        no hoarders
Will one get enlightenment
        without sitting under the bodhi tree
Will rice cook without fire
Will thirst quench without water
Will all deserts turn suddenly into oceans

Poor Man! What does he know
except to rearrange known words
twisting and turning them upside down in rows and rows

To look forward to is not new
If you come out
after looking forward yet again looking forward
here too you have to look forward endlessly

Shall we name life
    "Looking Forward"

(Translation of "Idettaa")

MYSELF

Holding me tight from all sides—
        the thought of making me utter a lie
The entire body is becoming a lump
Blood and flesh becoming one like squashed mass
Someone would come make tiny tiny balls
make them into rotis when people place orders

Even so not wanting to utter a lie
frying on and on on the skillet into someone's digestive system

How many plots to ensnare
How many nails have to be driven in—even so
one who is a human being is indeed a human being
Even if the iron-beaked crows
    peck and eat
he will not utter an untruth he will not burn in fire

If he thinks of something
he will not sleep till it is fulfilled

(Translation of "Nannu")

EQUIPOISE

I remember Vyoma I remember Sandhya
I remember Nalini Neeraja Radhamma
Each one has a sorrow-filled
        prison life
There are hot boiling lakes under their feet
Every morning
the sky and earth merging with them
becoming agitated
stuck in some broken branch—
Even so they
    calmly fully
    straightening their dishevelled hair with the hand
    over gardens over hills
    throwing an indifferent look
    slowly without the smile disappearing
how are they able to remain
What pure life skill
is able to keep them so fresh
Are they relatives of the water bird that
    drowns somewhere floats elsewhere
Perhaps casting aside the most heinous things
with the left hand
building a creativity within

I think they keep moving on
Looking at them I pick up
my heart that has slid down
They help create
some new meaning
some new beauty to life

Even if we wait two days
even if we wait two aeons
no semblance of being disturbed

(Translaion of "Samathookam")

FROM THE RIM OF SOME CLOUD

Who is the boy who is hanging on to the string
that has fallen from the edge of some cloud
and swinging between two hills—
Kicking this hill with this foot
kicking that hill with that foot
unbounded endlessly between two hills
    the shadow of the boy who is swinging
    moves like a bird in the valley
    the song of the valleys is trembling lightly
        on the dew soaked grass

He sits on the hump of the river
that is sliding further and further
He can grasp the hill and the sky
        like two birds
He can place the cot between night and day and lie down
Is he the message that
        the rising winds of the seven worlds have sent
He presents the earth
        with a new awakening and departs
He fills the waning sweetness loveliness
moon-like love and departs

Open your fists and look
you will see a swing in your palm
you will see a river flowing in the upper direction
you will also see a moon-boy
sliding on a river
        as if sliding on a snowy mountain
Men and women all being pregnant
will labour desiring to deliver
The shriek of delivery
against the outer space
will be heard like a beacon of light

*

By the time you wake up a calm dawn
will be sitting in front of you

(Translation of "Ye Mabbu Anchununcho")

I DREAM

I dream of tomorrow
    as if the ploughshare that's burning in the furnace
    is ploughing the land tomorrow—
I dream of tomorrow
I dream that tomorrow will be good
                                        will be fantastic—
That the seed that fell into the earth
will sprout tomorrow and will swallow the sun—
I dream
that the beggar who stands in front of the house
                                        ringing the bell
will become the great Siva
    and perform the thandava dance
I dream—
I dream

(Translation of "Kalagantaa")

A SPARK OF FIRE

Those days
he would keep poking the doused coal stove
hoping to light the chutta
in case he finds a spark of fire
Thinking that the stove is doused
when you remove the ash and throw it in the garbage
somewhere a spark would linger
burning the heap of garbage
With the ash from the stove
they would wash the dishes brush their teeth
all would shine

It's important that a spark should survive
be it in the stove or in the body
Body too is like the stove
It will burn as long as possible
If it gets extinguished it will happen just like that

(Translation of " Nippuravva")

UNABLE TO SLEEP AT NIGHT

He keeps reading the night in its entirety
        over the length of its parvas
        over the length of its skandhas[17]
As the night spreads in the form of yojanas
he would wage the Ramayana and the Mahabharata wars
                                                        simultaneously
One doesn't know during the day
that the night is so vast
that it is a primeval being that's born of the forest
What does not frighten us during the day
        would it frighten us during the night!
No, does it bestow knowledge
Wind is wind all sweet-smelling
delicate mellifluous voice—but
night becoming kinder
caressing most delicately
every body every single object—
like a medicinal touch—
How many sorrows how many pains how many hardships
all in a way go behind the curtain—
with peaceful nature with soothing kind patience
with the love of a long-standing step well

17 Parvas and skandhas refer to divisions in epics.

everything is nothing but pleasingly cool water—
O universal mother!
How many nights would you drop in my lap

How many nights
will I illumine
like a heartfelt song

(Translation of "Raatri Nidrapattaka")

REWARD

Days pass by
        happily or unhappily
        with hope or without hope
Do we provide wings to the days
The bird of all seasons will
fly everyday and become one with the wind
Beneath it we
see the time that struggles
having been caught in its claws
During summer the earth cracks
As soon as the first rains come everything moves
                                        and comes together
From within a bird will rise
Days slide—from your eyes
                        or from your fingers
Your body plateau blossoms
                        The chariot sets out
Crowds in great numbers along the chariot
beneath the clouds—in the sky
at the height of your outstretched hand flies a flag
Perhaps your hand itself transforms into the flag
I bend each day
like a flower and smell it

I don't pluck it it loses its beauty when plucked
Enjoying without destroying worshipping it
is how we give each day its reward

(Translation of "Bahumaanam")

OUR HOUSES

When I look at our houses
I am reminded
of crab holes
Perhaps
        losing freedom
begins only with the house—
House is nothing but getting stuck in the narrow space of the hole
from the spacious world
Security—protection—
        empty words
Do words depict our circumstances—
        write about them?

(Translation of "Mana Illu")

BEHIND THE NETS

I'm walking all but dangerously
amongst dangerous moments
Dangerous life every moment—
Every moment a landmine
A pleasure trip between moments of a landmine
Don't know when which one will blast
A life used to blasts—
A life that doesn't have any instruments
to locate the landmines—
Like scattering millets for pigeons
all the lures only behind the nets outside—

(Translation of "Valala Venaka")

ABOUT THE TRANSLATORS

M. Sridhar and Alladi Uma have been translating for over twenty five years. Among their translations are *Ayoni and Other Stories* published by Katha, New Delhi, G. Kalyana Rao's *Untouchable Spring* published by Orient Blackswan and K. Siva Reddy's *Mohana! Oh Mohana! and Other Poems* (Sahitya Akademi). They taught English and retired from the University of Hyderabad.